NARCISSISM
The Killer of Love

STEVEN K CRAIG

www.steven-k-craig.com

Printed in the United States of America

ISBN-13: 978-1492280415
ISBN-10: 1492280410

10 9 8 7 6 5 4 3 2 1

White Roses Publishing

www.steven-k-craig.com

INTRODUCTION

If you are reading this booklet, chances are you have recently been made aware that you've had your life ripped apart and turned upside down from being in a relationship with a Narcissist, and you are looking for some sort of understanding as to what has happened to you. No one has an interest in learning about the true nature of the beast, the Psychopathic Narcissist, unless he or she has been exposed to one, and when that happens, it's too late, the damage has already been done. Knowing this, my heart aches for you reading this. I know what you are experiencing right now. The agony, confusion, betrayal, and sense of great loss are almost too much to bear. I would not wish this torment to the heart, mind, and soul on anyone.

There is a Narcissist Epidemic taking place and it is a subject that can no longer be ignored. I put this booklet together with excerpts from my book Ghost of a Rose, and added more material not in the book. If you are just becoming aware of Narcissism, you can spend countless hours researching it on the Internet. However, if you are needing help understanding it quickly because you are confused and in pain, this booklet is meant to answer your questions and shed light on what is or has happened to you right now. It contains vital information that you need right now.

After reading this booklet, I recommend that you read my book Ghost of a Rose. It is my memoir, and a detailed account from beginning to end of my relationship and discovery of a Narcissist in real time, as it happened. As of date, therapists are little help to victims in overcoming Narcissistic Spousal Abuse. In the book, I outline what it took for me to overcome the damage done to my psyche, completely heal, and repair my heart and soul in order to trust and wholly love again. You will not find the unique healing process I did to return my heart to an age of innocence anywhere else.

I know you are hurting right now. You feel as if you have no future and that the pain will never go away. It may not help at the moment, but I want you to know, I lost everything during and after my relationship with a Narcissist. I was taken to the deepest, darkest depths where no man or woman should ever go, and was to the point of taking my own life. I lost my business, my

The Narcissist is **Exploitative** of others (e.g. takes advantage of others to achieve their own needs. Projects his/her faults on to others. He or she blames everyone for his or her behavior and is never at fault. He or she puts on a good front (persona) to impress and exploit others).

The Narcissist **Lacks empathy** (e.g. is unwilling to recognize or identify with the feelings and needs of others. He or she does not care about the consequences of his/her actions, with little, if any conscience. The Narcissist is insensitive to the needs and feelings of others. He or she has no remorse for mistakes or misdeeds).

A Narcissist is often **Envious** of others or believes that others are envious of him or her. Seldom expresses appreciation, and seeks to hurt or destroy the objects of his or her frustration.

The Narcissist regularly shows **arrogant, haughty behaviors or attitudes.** (e.g., unreliable, undependable, and pathological lying. He or she is not interested in problem solving, and does not listen because they do not care. He or she feels misunderstood, and always has a hidden agenda.

An intimate relationship with a pathological Narcissist will shake the foundation of faith and rattle the soul so sadistically that the shattered heart and tormented mind questions the very existence of God, and some victims of the Narcissist's rein of torture end up losing belief all together in the aftermath. It is one of the closest things to Hell on Earth.

I can attest to this and several survivors I have talked with will do the same. I went into my relationship with a Narcissist having a faithful belief in God, and afterwards, it was stripped from me. A relationship with a psychopath will change everything about a person and strip even the strongest of all self-worth. It will put to test a person's ability to survive and take away the capability to function normally. It will destroy trust and push the mind to the edge of insanity.

If the Narcissist wants the stimulation of an intimate relationship, he/she will stay in it as long as the relationship excites him/her. Wanting to appear normal and respectful, he or she may even go as far as getting married.

Narcissists are skillfully manipulative and extremely charming. It is almost impossible to say no to them. They lure their target with promises of undying love and offer them whatever has been missing in their life. They offer passion and romance on a scale far above normal, and a close friendship that is impossible to resist. If a person is experiencing financial difficulties, the Narcissist will even offer money just to seem generous.

During the "honeymoon" phase, the Narcissist pours on the charm to hook the victim emotionally and gain his or her trust. They present themselves as kind-hearted, caring individuals, and in order to manipulate the chosen target, they resort to outrageous lies. In romantic relationships in particular, the Narcissist depicts him or herself completely compatible with the victim, creating the illusion of a soul mate. The Narcissist claims to share the same interests and sensibilities. They transform themselves into a mirror image of the victim.

When the Narcissists goal is seducing a target, his or her pursuit feels like an idealization, creating the illusion of a soul mate to the person snared in the trap. Temporarily, the victim represents the object of the Narcissist's desire. The victim feels as if the Narcissist is the answer to his or her needs, the love of their life, and the key to their happiness. However, this feeling of euphoria does not last long because it is empty to the core.

Not all Narcissists enter a relationship with a hidden agenda. Some of them honestly want to be in a loving relationship, but in time, his or her true nature emerges. They are truly a Dr. Jekyll and Mr. Hyde. It begins as a fantasy for the Narcissist, but the truth is, they are incapable of love for anyone other than themselves.

Narcissists take the term "love yourself" to a pathological level. They are so self absorbed that there is little left to give someone else. They will go through the motions, but it's only an act, and only for personal gain. They don't feel for others the way normal people do. The Narcissist is incapable of compassion. Their deceiving, shallow soul is what blindsides the victim after believing that he or she had a loving relationship. When the romantic relationship is at an all time high, all of a sudden, the Narcissist does an about face and discards the victim without any warning. It's hard to grasp, but you must understand that it was not personal, and that the Narcissist cannot love anyone except him or herself.

The Narcissist inflicts extreme pain and abuse on others. They devalue their sources of supply, callously abandon, and discard people, places, partnerships, relatives, and friendships unhesitatingly. Sudden shifts between sadism and altruism, abuse and love, ignoring and caring, abandoning and clinging, viciousness and remorse, the harsh and the tender, are perhaps the most difficult to comprehend and to accept. The Narcissist will profess undying love, and then suddenly, the victim cannot do anything right and nothing is good enough for the Narcissist.

The Narcissist appears so beautiful, handsome, sweet, and caring, only to dry up and vanish like a ghost as if they never existed. They forget the victim in the blink of an eye, and then seasonally blooming like a rose, the victim reaches for it, but is left with prickly thorns and trickling blood. Once a gaping wound is open, they disappear again, a soul with no footprints.

I am going to repeat this several times in this booklet, so it may sink in about Narcissists, and as difficult as it is to comprehend, these people have no empathy, no conscience, and absolutely no remorse. As a victim, you must keep reminding yourself of this fact.

A Narcissist acts irrational and they do not see the world as you or I. They are dangerous because they have no feelings for anyone but themselves. The words "sorry" and "love" are just tools for them to get what they want, and they enjoy nothing more than shattering lives for a sense of power. Once they have depleted the very essence of life out of their victim, they move onto the next and never look back. It's almost impossible for a person with empathy to grasp that someone who claimed to be the love of his or her life, never actually loved them at all.

Narcissists are easily and perpetually bored. When you question anything, say, or do the 'wrong' thing, its game over, and they quickly come to despise you. You're human and not perfect, so it's only a matter of when, not if, that you fall from that pedestal; even if you are aware of it and cater to the Narcissist by working at keeping up with his or her need for supply. No matter what you do, they seem to require a constant supply of 'new' adulation."

The Narcissist's favorite form of torment is "The Silent Treatment." This comes after the abandonment. The Narcissist's aim is to silence communication. More specifically, it's to render the victim invisible, a non-entity, and in so doing, making the victim powerless. It is deeply disturbing to be silenced by someone you love and someone you believed loved you.

This "Silent Treatment" that is the tactical technique of torture by a Narcissist is not the same as a normal person just being upset for a short time. The silent treatment by a Narcissist is a statement of contempt, "You aren't worth the energy it would take me to acknowledge your existence, let alone your feelings or needs." The silent treatment is one of the worst forms of the psychopaths' abuse because they are driving the victim to emotional instability, and for some, in a direction to end their life, especially after many years of investment in him/her by having a family and building a future.

Without warning, the Narcissist abandons all that he/she pretended to care for and love, and then refuses to speak. The Narcissist's trait is to abandon the ones that love them the most.

Narcissists must feed their need for admiration and self-importance. This is referred to as Narcissistic Supply. When they are filling themselves with narcissistic supply, they will push everyone off to the side, as he or she does with intimate relationships, family, friends, and even their children. The victim is a source of supply, but eventually he or she will need a new source and immediately end the relationship and move forward as if the person never existed. Once the victim stops serving that purpose, he or she is discarded as though they have never existed. Some Narcissists commit what is referred to as Mental Murder. They simply ostracize the victim that was convinced to believe in undying love. The Narcissist ignores the existence of the victim and will not ever speak his or her name. To them, they have killed the victim off, leaving him or her, a non-entity. In fact, they will avoid looking at him or her even if they are sitting directly in front of them.

Healthy relationships do not end abruptly with one person acting as if it never even happened. Normal people cannot detach so quickly from deep emotional ties. Healthy relationships are not based on emotional abuse, domination, and a mountain of deliberate lies and manipulation, and this is the foundation of all relationships with a Narcissist.

A romantic relationship with a Narcissist changes the brain chemicals in the victim, causing depression, confusion, and a sense of worthlessness that could lead the victim to end it all. Narcissist abuse is just as deadly as cancer and heart disease as many victims commit suicide or withdrawal to die a slow, painful death, the Perfect Murder.

In almost every case study, the victim was a strong, assertive, active, and happy individual going into the relationship. The Narcissist seeks out highly sensitive people to victimize because a person less empathetic will quickly see through the façade. However, the aftermath of a highly sensitive person's relationship with a Narcissist is a life left in ruins, financially, mentally, and emotionally. It changes and scars the victim into becoming a different person, whom also could end up suffering with Post Traumatic Stress Disorder. PTSD is not a disorder that solely happens to those serving the military in a combat situation as you may have heard on televised news reports. It is an infliction brought forth as the result of psychological trauma to the psyche. However, even after a person has been completely destroyed by a Narcissist, the torment is far from over. If you are involved with a Narcissist, prepare yourself because you are about to have a front seat on the most crazy roller coaster ride of your life. The Narcissist comes back for more, and continues to do so until there is nothing remaining of the person that he or she once claimed to love.

The degree of PTSD varies from person to person. It can occur during an abusive relationship and long after it has ended. Leading Narcissism specialist Sam Vaknin writes, "A relationship with a narcissist is a never-ending story. Even the official termination of a relationship with a Narcissist is not the end of the affair. In the Narcissists mind, the ex belongs to them. He or she is an inseparable part of their Pathological

Narcissistic Space. This possessive streak survives the physical separation." Abuse is not limited to physical and can extend far into emotional. The events that take place in a relationship with a Narcissist fall outside the range of "normal" human experiences. The victim suffers with delayed and protracted intrusive responses that are so debilitating that they prevent ordinary day-to-day life and hamper the ability to function normally.

Once the ideal mate suddenly turns to a cold, callous, emotionless, devaluing, sadistic, manipulative individual the torment is just beginning. After long-term exposure to this form abuse, the victim suffers from flashbacks, nightmares, sleep disturbances, avoidance of certain places and activities, emotional numbness, detachment, high anxiety, depression, and suicidal thoughts; all of this just because he or she loved someone that has no ability to love.

You may be asking yourself how someone could be in love with such a monster. Psychopaths are intuitively skilled at giving just enough validation and attention to keep a victim on a hook. It's as if the psychopath instinctively knows when to be charming in order not to lose the victim as a source of much needed Narcissistic Supply.

The tormenting actions of the Narcissist are buried deep inside the victim's psyche, and haunt him or her long after the end of the relationship. In my case, as part of the PTSD, the daily nightmares would not go away. Each dream had her seek me out and convince me that she is the love of mine, and her, life. After the forth abandonment, my guard was up, but she knew how to penetrate it, and once I let her in, she proceeded to cruelly rip my heart out before abandoning me once again. I experienced hundreds of these scenarios, and woke up screaming, "Get out of my head!" That's when I finally began to get mad and hate her for what she's done. I became upset with myself when love turned to hate, but that is what comes of having your soul raped repeatedly. The nightmares would not go away. I tried sleeping pills and staying awake until I reached complete exhaustion. Nothing worked, and no matter how hard or what I tried, my mind was invaded by them every day around 4am. At one point, I felt as if I was going crazy. My biggest desire in life was to find real love, and I thought I had that with Ashley. I had a hard time accepting that soulless people, such as her, exist.

PTSD is the gift Ashley gave me for loving her, and healing from it was harder than I could have imagined. A chronic drug user struggling to break free of their long-term addiction has it easier. It took years for me to come out of the deep depression of losing the woman I loved. The first step is coming to terms with the reality that you as the victim have been or are being manipulated and used.

When exiting a relationship with a Narcissist, you must face the fact that the person you considered your soul mate is, in fact, a ruthless psychopath, an illusion of perfection that they created to manipulate you. As a victim, and as hard as it is to accept, you must come to terms with the fact that they never really loved you.

A Narcissist will eventually devalue and discard the victim with no remorse. It's inevitable in any relationship with a Narcissist. At some point, he or she will emotionally and physically withdraw and leave a now broken person wondering what he or she did wrong.

Even after the final separation, I stayed in a state of denial. As with all victims, he or she defends and makes excuses for the actions of his or her Narcissist. I fought for love with everything I had in me, but there is not a soul on earth that can penetrate the darkness within her, and this is what you need to know about the Narcissist if you have one in your life. In the course of the battle to save love, I lost myself.

Over the next few years, I struggled to find a way back from having my soul raped, and a new war was waged as I fought not to give up on life or become jaded, numb of any feelings, and remain alone for the rest of my life. This turned out to be the toughest battle of all. The turning point for me was when I realized Ashley used my daughter as a tool to get to me. She lied to my daughter and manipulated her to get what she wanted, and no one is allowed to do that to my daughter, regardless of my feelings towards them.

The world is crowded with people suffering from NPD and the numbers are increasing at an alarming rate. Almost all specialists will tell you to run, but for those caught up in a relationship with a Narcissist, it's not that easy. In fact, it's extremely difficult to separate yourself from the Narcissist. The victim only remembers the good times and desperately wants to return to those days of blissful feelings. Don't live in denial as I did. You cannot save or help a Narcissist. It's a battle that cannot be won. The damage that these people cause is catastrophic and you will not come out of it unscathed.

As a victim, you might be taken to the point of not wanting to live anymore due to the loss of the soul mate illusion. Just know this, if you were to die, the Narcissist may have a slight feeling sorrow for a brief moment (although highly doubtful), but the Narcissist simply fabricates justification, moves on, and never looks back. The Narcissist has in fact, figured out how to achieve the perfect murder. Men and women alike have committed suicide due to a relationship with a Narcissist, and no one ever knows why he or she took their own life. The Narcissist may not pull the trigger, but is guilty of emotionally murdering a person with no remorse or conscience. If you are at that dreadful point feeling that there is no reason to go on, stop it! It is all a sick, twisted game to the Narcissist. If you were to take your own life, the Narcissist wins the grand prize. Do not give them that. Don't let them win. Stand up, fight back, and be the victor by becoming happy again. It is the best revenge because your happiness turns the table on them and drives Narcissists crazy.

A person may never fully recover from Narcissistic abuse unless he or she is determined to do so. I know the monster that lies within her (my Narcissist), but to this day, I still have a difficult time accepting what she is. How can any human completely lack empathy for another? It's a hard fact to comprehend. After reflecting back on every moment we were together to write the book Ghost of a Rose, it was a rude awakening as I realized that Ashley never, and I mean, not once did she ever show compassion towards my feelings. It was always about hers and hers alone.

I've asked myself thousands of times, "Why me? All I wanted was to love her. I did everything right and gave whatever she needed. What did I do to deserve this?" All my life I've been in pursuit of real love and I thought I'd finally found it. That love turned out to be nothing more than a cruel joke.

Deborah Ward explained it best when she wrote, "For someone on the outside looking at a relationship between a highly sensitive person (HSP) and a Narcissist, it's all too easy to blame the sensitive one. How and why would anyone want to stay in such a relationship? Surely, it was obvious that this person was taking you for a ride, but of course, it is not always obvious. Long-standing Narcissistic behavior is not always immediately apparent and the Narcissist often becomes highly skilled at getting what they want through charm, deception, passive-aggression, control tactics, and manipulation. Narcissists feel they are superior to other people, although it may manifest itself in subtle ways, such as complaining about hotel service or ignoring expert advice. They are preoccupied with achieving success, power, beauty, fame, and wealth, although whatever they do achieve is never enough. They have a complete lack of empathy for others, including their own family, children, and friends, so they will take advantage of people to get their own needs and desires met, even if it hurts someone. The HSP doesn't consciously choose this kind of relationship, but they are particularly vulnerable to it."

I was a prime target for a Narcissist because many of them seek a person of high stature. They want this in a partner for nothing more than to make themselves look good in the eyes of others. Ashley chose me because of the glamorous, out-of-the-ordinary lifestyle I led. What's twisted about this is, eventually such a person repulses the Narcissist because they cannot reach a high level of success on their own, and this is when the Narcissist begins to devalue the other person.

Narcissists are prone to be workaholics, but unlike those that work hard to enhance life, the Narcissist only strives for power and craves being the center of attention. They use manipulation tactics in order to get people to serve them while attempting to achieve their goal. They will say anything, name-drop, and do whatever is needed to simply impress others. A Narcissist needs to be admired and shows no empathy or concern for the feelings of other people, but they are skilled at making their peers believe that they do have compassion. Narcissists constantly flirt for attention, and most will cheat during a relationship. Narcissism specialist Sam Vaknin breaks it down to two categories concerning sex and the Narcissist. The Cerebral Narcissist has no problem remaining celibate; they prefer to masturbate rather than seek sex. A Somatic

Narcissist is just the opposite because they have no problem screwing anyone. They have sex without emotion and use the partner as a warm, pulsating vibrator.

The driving force behind Narcissists is admiration and greed. Most are exceedingly greedy, and are constantly planning and scheming, even in their sleep, about how to expand their power base. You may not see it on the surface, but the Narcissist hungers for everything out of reach: money, property, power, adulation, fame, and dominance over the lives of others. An unconscious bottomless pit of psychological emptiness drives narcissistic greed. In some Narcissists, the greed grows so strongly that these individuals destroy the lives of others to get what they want. However, they lack skill and are under qualified because they cannot be bothered with obtaining an academic degree or professional training. They just run around in circles. As confusing as it is, when a Narcissist is offered a business opportunity, he or she can't fake their way through, they recoil and obstruct every stage of the negotiations, and then bail. They are unable to work as a team, compromise, and work towards long term goals. The Narcissist trait is to be superior to others and once anyone gets close enough to see their imperfections, they run. They do this as a necessity in order to view themselves as perfect and not be seen for their flaws.

As the Narcissist's arrogance builds, the illusion of grandeur affects all areas of their life, and the lives of those closest to them. It is inevitable that the Narcissist fails, and as confidence wanes, growing insecurity causes them to criticize their spouse in order to regain the superior position in the relationship. The Narcissist believes that he or she is above the law and societal rules, which leads them to unethical and immoral behavior. They lose their integrity by committing outrageous acts of lying, stealing, fraud, and infidelity. Projection of blame and even dissociation gives these self-serving individuals license to be unfaithful, in order to feed their sagging egos. It matters not whom gets hurt in the process, and this is a never-ending cycle with a Narcissist. Narcissists live in a world of total chaos, and are unable to commit to anything or anyone for a long period.

Some Narcissists just laze about and engage in trivial pursuits, seeking entertainment and excitement wherever he or she can, while living off others in parasitic form.

You are not the first, and will not be the last. Narcissists and psychopaths suffer incurable personality disorders, and repeat the same relationship cycle, no matter whom they are having a relationship with or for how long. Its seemingly ideal beginning will invariably have a bitter ending.

Narcissists feel compelled to change in times of crisis, as Ashley did when she thought she could lose me (her ultimate Narcissistic Supply) forever, or when they are starved of that supply. They will pour on the charm, and once the supply is available again, they will revert to his or her true self. Even though I was aware of her narcissism, I was not strong enough walk away, and I found myself asking (begging) her to get back together with me. That was my biggest mistake. A Narcissist feeds on the misery of other people. When they see you are "desperately" in love with them, you have just given them the ultimate Narcissistic Supply. This makes them feel in control and they enjoy it when he or she can discard and reject you at any given time. They are able to toy with you, as they feel fit by either discarding you or mercifully allowing you to be with them again.

After the Narcissist abandons the victim, it's far from over and the abuse will continue. As is the Narcissist's protocol, he or she will periodically resurface. They give a moment of value, and even a glimpse of the "pretend person." This provides the Narcissist with a sense of power and now constantly devalues the victim. This will go on as long as it amuses the Narcissist. The constant abandonment will continue to take place for no reason, only to come back month's later professing undying love before bailing again. This almost drove me insane. If I had been paying attention, she told me herself that she did this to her ex-husband, whom she first abandoned two months after they were married and preceded to do so many times during the relationship. The signs were all there. I just did not see them, because either I didn't want to or she was just that good at manipulating me. It is sadistic to devalue a person that has given their love time after time.

When the victim is completely drained dry, the Narcissist vanishes. Time passes and the victim struggles to put his or her life back together and rebuild their self-esteem. Then out of nowhere, the Narcissist returns. The victim wants to know what they did wrong and apologizes, once again assuming all the blame. The Narcissist adores this since he or she feels better than everyone else. The victim is led into believing that everything will be all right, but it will not be. The Narcissist has flair for the dramatic and when his or her mask is on, they are truly a wolf in sheep's clothing. The Narcissist is not back for reconciliation; they are back to twist the knife again, and feed off the victim. It took 2 years of this torment before I finally had enough and called her out for what she is. Then came the final discard, and the torture stopped. Angry because her power was taken away, she became furious and revolted by fabricating monstrous lies to justify her abandonment. In her mind, she became the victim and tried to convince everyone around her that she was.

She kept me hanging on by a thread for years. Finally, I was made aware of the illness, and once I learned everything about it, I came to realize there is no saving her, or us. Ashley had said many times, "It will never be over between us." That may have been true if I never knew the Narcissist game, and when her mask fell and I saw her true self, it was my choice to end the relationship, not hers this time. Since then, I have talked with a few victims that have been going back and forth with their Narcissist for close to 30 years. Narcissism is their life sentence. It's not yours. Do not allow this to happen to you.

When my Narcissist claimed it would never be over between us, it was a statement of empty words. It's part of what is referred to as "Gaslighting." Gaslighting is a Tango performed by the Narcissist and is a form of psychological warfare that is deliberate in nature. This is what is most prevalent to my story. It involves an insidious set of psychological manipulations that are carried out gradually in stages, and repeated time after time, in order to undermine the mental stability of its victim.

Stage 1: Idealization

This is when the Narcissist puts on their best face in order to lure the victim. They shower the victim with love, charm, passion, and make promises of a never-ending love. They mirror the victim in every way as to give the illusion of the ideal love and portray the soul mate concept. Caught up in an alluring state of euphoria, the victim enjoys every moment of the honeymoon stage and believes the partner feels the same, but this is the Narcissist's biggest deception.

Stage 2: Devaluation

Almost overnight the Narcissist becomes decisively cold, callus, and uncaring. Their words turn cruel, criticizing, and devaluing in every possible way. Completely confused, the victim has no idea what's happening as they experience anxiety and depression. The roller-coaster relationship puts the victim in a constant state of chaos, and they frantically try to find a way back to when all was good. The victim is forced to focus on defending themselves from a barrage of accusations by the Narcissist. At this point, there is no reasoning with the Narcissist. When the Narcissist no longer gets the positive attention that they crave, they resort to ostracizing and stop all communication. Confused by the Narcissists behavior, the victim works harder to please them with the hope of getting the relationship back where it began. Alone and isolated from the real world, unable to cope with the abandonment and rejection, the victim falls into a deep pit of depression, and sometimes become suicidal. Even though the Narcissist despises the victim for what they have become, they are still a source of supply, and it's far from over. The Narcissist will return in a macabre dance. Herein lays a paradox because the more a victim shows distress, the more they become a form of Narcissistic supply. They initiate the push-pull game. This is a way of holding onto their supply by saying, "I hate you. Leave me alone" to "I love you. Don't ever leave me." This pushes the victim to the edge of insanity.

Stage 3: Discarding

This is when the Narcissist's game comes to an end. At this point, the once proclaimed "love of a lifetime" is done with the victim that has outlived their usefulness. It's time to move on and find another source of supply. The victim is then discarded in a brutally cold and emotionless manner. They are ostracized as the

Narcissist cuts off any and all communication. In the Narcissists mind, the victim never existed.

For more information on Gaslighting read "The Effects of Gaslighting in Narcissistic Victim Abuse" by Christine Louis de Canonville.

Gaslighting is a form of brainwashing, and this is what makes it almost impossible to break free from the spell of a Narcissist. When someone says to move on, it's not as cut and dry as they think. They speak blindly without knowledge, when the victim is in the throes of the greatest mind-fuck and soul rape conceivable, nothing can break the spell. It's not just a "toxic" relationship; it's insanity in the raw.

No matter what you may think or how much you try, a Narcissist cannot be saved or cured. Narcissism is not a disease that is contracted. It's not a chemical imbalance. It's not something they are born with. Narcissism is a mental illness that is created. A Narcissist cannot be cured because they view themselves as perfect. To them, it is everyone else that is flawed. When and how did the Narcissist epidemic begin? That is a good question. Society is breeding them like maggots in a sewer. They are the partial creation of an entertainment media gone mad that has no accountability for the immoral idiocy they produce. There is now four causes linked to the mass creation of Narcissists, which are parenting or the lack of, celebrity trash culture, unaccountable media and Internet, and easy credit (not so easy now). For example, parents attempt to raise children with self-esteem. Many parents tell their children that he or she is the best there is and will treat them as royalty. This is fine to a certain degree, but parents are taking it too far by instilling an entitlement mentality. This leads to Narcissism. The celebrity trash culture is a breeding ground for narcissism. MTV with its reality shows such as Jersey Shore and Girl Code are major culprits. Reality shows in general are highly narcissistic, as are most celebrities. What they really are is a showcase for narcissistic people and behavior that makes narcissism seems normal. The entertainment media promotes narcissism and the Internet is the breeding ground for it. Take Facebook and Instagram where people constantly post photos of themselves, saying, "look at me." Last, but not least is, or was, is readily available easy credit. This allowed to people to purchase material items way out of there means. It allowed men to purchase lavish toys and women to recreate themselves with plastic surgery.

Narcissists are the worst of the worse. They should be locked up to rot in solitaire. Betty LaLuna who operates a website entitled Narcraiders, says, "A Narcissist can watch you drown and eat a cheeseburger at the same time. These are very sick people that are looking to swallow you up whole, and no amount of love will repair these fixer-uppers. The Narcissist character has been permanently foreclosed. Accept the bankruptcy and keep moving." As unbelievable as this may sound, it is true. Specialists cannot stress enough that the Narcissist has no empathy for anyone. They are skilled at convincing you otherwise, but it's all a façade.

How to spot a Narcissist

It is nearly impossible to spot or profile a Narcissist as a preemptive measure to avoid one, and when you do, it's too late. Here are more of the traits to look for as early warning signs.

- Overly charming in the beginning

- Illusions of grandeur
- He or she projects feelings of insecurities
- Emotion-phobia
- A fragmented family story
- A need for control
- Idol worship
- Never at fault
- No emotional support
- Always the victim
- Never admits to being wrong
- Everything is about him or her
- Silent treatments and neglect can and do go on for several weeks at a time, especially if you point out one of his or her flaws.
- While you do everything possible for your relationship, he or she does nothing.
- Name drops
- Alienates spouse from friends
- Angers easily
- Baits and picks fights
- Falsely accuses
- Domestic theft
- Dissociation from reality

- Denial
- Imposed isolation
- Neglect
- Shaming
- Stalking

One red flag to look for is the lack of close friends. Narcissists have many acquaintances, but no close friends to speak of. They cannot be close to people for long periods because the mask will eventually slip and his or her true self will be seen.

Even with all that we know, there really is no way to profile a narcissist. It's very scary out there now if you are not trained what to look for. The body language is there, you just have to look and listen. Although, for the untrained eye, they won't know until it's too late.

The victim is nothing more to the Narcissist than a glance at a dying animal on the side of the road with its guts spilling out. This was obvious to me when I had a gun to my head, seconds away from pulling the trigger, and she waited 4 hours before calling my father to have him check to see if I was alive after she hung up the phone on me. If I would have pulled the trigger, she simply would have dismissed it and moved on as if I never existed, which is exactly what she ended up doing anyway.

Characteristics of a Victim
with a Narcissistic Lover

- You are constantly confused about partner's sudden changes in behavior.
- You never knowing what might happen next.
- You feel forced to "walk on eggshells".
- You come home to find Dr. Jekyll and suddenly discovering Mr. Hyde, and never knowing what caused the change.
- You are always apologizing for things that are never your fault.
- You make up stories to friends and family about to justify their actions.
- Blaming yourself for never doing things well enough for the other.
- Never completely trusting your partner.
- Never feeling respected or equal in the relationship.

- Always worrying about your performance in any role, including in the bedroom.
- Not being allowed free access to their financial accounts.
- Not being able to give your opinion for fear of being chastised.
- You are never able to win an argument.
- Always wondering what you did "wrong".
- You avoid arguments at all costs.
- Always attempting to "try harder" to make things better.
- Chronically feeling empty.
- May periodically have suicidal thoughts.
- Wishing for "someday" when things will change, but someday never comes.
- After breaking up with their narcissistic partner, all they want to do is run back to them.
- Repeatedly making excuses for and forgiving your partner's unacceptable behaviors, which continue to happen.
- Always told everything is your fault.
- Often feeling humiliated by your partner.

- Constantly fearing abandonment by your partner, so "doing whatever it takes" to keep him or her.
- Doing things they are uncomfortable with because you feel pressured to do so.
- Compromising values, needs, and beliefs because your partner wants you to.
- Discovering that the narcissist has frequently lied or misled you.
- Feeling like no one else could possibly love you as intensely as the Narcissists soul mate illusion.
- Feeling subservient or less-than your partner.
- Rarely feeling like their needs are being met or even acknowledged.
- Often wishing you would have never gotten into this mess to begin with and now don't know how to get out.
- Frequently feel numb or depressed.
- They no longer know who you really are.
- You may end up looking like the "crazy one" in the relationship.

all their relationships fail miserably. Just be thankful that you are free from their reign of terror.

The only way to completely be rid of the Narcissist is to come to terms with the reality that you were used, manipulated, and lied to. Nothing was real. Your pain does not evoke any sympathy in a Narcissist. If you show any sign of weakness, you are only making your situation worse, and a Narcissist gets more supply when he or she can reject you in a cold, cruel way. No matter how much you want to believe, you never actually mattered to them. A relationship to them is nothing more than a jolt of Narcissistic Supply, a place to live for a while, a need to be admired or for sex.

There is nothing wrong with admitting to having been conned, and there is no shame to it. What are you guilty of? Being loving, kind, compassionate, and empathetic to someone who clearly can't return those things? It's sad that all the victim wanted was to love them, and what makes matters worse is when the victim begins to see the truth. They really do hate it when you start to unravel the truth as to who they really are. They will not admit to it, but they develop contempt and hatred towards the victim for really seeing them for the monsters they are.

For anyone who questions the integrity of the victim of a Narcissist, just look at the other people they manipulate: judges, attorneys, counselors, family members, friends, children, etc. We cannot truthfully answer why they exist, nor can we fix them, but we can heal, and we can survive.

Thanks to the dedicated work of specialists, I was able to move on knowing that there was nothing wrong with me. There never was. Everything I did; how I reacted, thought, felt, behaved, and respond was pervasive patterns to the mental and emotional abuse I was subjected to. There is a new diagnosis in the DSM for this now called "Victim of Narcissistic Abuse Syndrome."

We can have the last laugh by truly experiencing love, life, and happiness. A Narcissist will never be able to embrace that gift. One of the many times she bailed on us, Ashley made the comment, "You lose." No, actually, I won. You can only lose if something had value to it.

No matter which way the relationship ends it's always messy and left with unfinished business that cannot be resolved like a "normal" relationship. What's frightening is, they are doing it to someone else right now. The Narcissist quickly moves onto find a new source of Narcissistic Supply, and the nightmare begins for another man or woman that is the next in line to be victimized.

Be very careful long after the relationship is over. The narcissistic psychopath has a tenancy for coming back if you were good source of Narcissistic Supply. In addition, the Narcissist is a master chess player and does not like to lose. When the Narcissist is not being fed his or her much-needed supply, they will reflect back and stalk you. The Internet and everyone engaging in social media outlets has made this very easy to do. They are sneaky in their cyber stalking, but so predictable because they all follow the same pattern. Take Facebook for example. The Narcissist will block you from viewing his or her profile, but will have a second account under a different name to spy on you. My relationship with a Narcissist has been over for many years, but I see her ip address viewing my personal website still today. It's actually kind of funny to me now because I know when she is between men.

In the end, all the manipulation and the people whose lives they have damaged will have been for nothing. His or her life will end bitter, alone, and loveless. As for me, and hopefully you as well, I'm going to find that one special person that is waiting for me, and we will share a real, unconditional, spectacular, and magnificent love. And this is the healthy conclusion of an unhealthy relationship.

There is no doubt my path to understanding would have been longer, or non-existent without the help of others. I am no longer the innocent who tried to be happy despite my ignorance. My understanding came at a personal price; I had to give up my dreams of a perfect love. Although, good can come from the worst experiences. I'm out there, searching to find those caught in the throes of a psychopathic relationship.

If you are searching for help online, be very careful when joining or engaging in websites (especially facebook pages) that focus on narcissistic abuse. I have checked into most of the online forums, most are informative and helpful, but be wary of those that are

how to love and it is why they are chosen to be victimized by the Narcissist.

Everyone concentrates on the negative of Narcissistic abuse, and rightfully so. They have had their life left in ruins, suffer from PTSD, and have been exposed to the underbelly of real evil. Yes, I said "Evil" and although many will argue that statement, what else would you call them? These individuals have total contempt and rage for those exposing the truth. It makes them irate because how could an inferior person ever be able to match their far superior Narcissistic personality, especially since they have already been devalued and discarded. Narcissists lack the ability to recognize what they have done to others, and cannot own up what liars they are. They fool everyone on the outside of their homes and especially other family members and keep their victims isolated and imprisoned. These abusers are only one-step away from a psychopath murderer. They are destroying countless individuals, families, and children.

John Carpenter (writer/director) of the horror movie Halloween was asked in an interview to describe the mass murdering character Michael Myers. He said the

Michael is pure evil. His description of pure evil is someone that has no empathy, no conscience, and no remorse.   These are the same traits as that of the pathological Narcissist/Sociopath.

As a psychopath, they should be held accountable for the destruction they create, and hopefully someday, courts of law will finally recognize these soulless creatures for how truly dangerous they are. Unfortunately, if you were to bring up Narcissism in a court of law, it would be thrown out because the courts do not recognize the illness. The Narcissist is so skilled at putting on a convincing act that it is almost impossible to detect unless you were the one caught in their trap.

The Narcissist has finally been given the title they deserve, and it is that of a psychopath. The more people are educated they will be able to spot these dangerous predators, and people will start to take them and their victims more seriously.

There is light at the end of the tunnel, and once the victim has healed, they will seek real love. When they do find that special someone that can truly love in return, a real fairytale romance will take place. How lucky is it for a person to have the love of a Narcissistic abuse survivor? Very lucky! The chosen will experience love on a level that they have only dreamed of and thought impossible. Unlike the Narcissist, the love you have to give is real. It hurts knowing that our Narcissist immediately moved on to another sucker to feed off, but we all know he or she will finish out his or her life in misery. Don't let them win by becoming jaded and closed off. They crave knowledge of the pain they have caused. Take control and be the one to win. Don't be scared, open your heart, and let the love flow. Your next lover is going to feel they have won the lottery with you. As a survivor, you appreciate love, and are capable of giving more than a great deal of people on earth.

God Created Narcissists

When it concerns narcissism, I think we are overlooking something that may be very important to understand what makes these people who they are. The search for the answers as to how and why these abnormally destructive people exist has brought forth conclusions based on analysis from psychological studies, and that viewpoint is coming up short of a clear-cut and undeniable ruling, which leads you to believe that most of what we are hearing is still speculation. I think we need to look deeper and from a different angle to find a true understand to the Narcissistic epidemic that is currently taking place. As of to date, no explanation for their being is set in stone. We know how they perform, their traits, manipulation tactics, and the outcome of a relationship with a Narcissist, but what makes them who they are? No one really knows for certain what causes these disordered people to be void of empathy and lack all moral fiber. It's obvious that these twisted individuals are missing something in human structure.

Psychologists refrain from using the word "evil" when describing a person with Narcissistic personality disorder because they don't acknowledge the existence of the spiritual realm, you know, science verses religion, both trying to discredit the other, but how else can someone that seemingly has no heart or soul, no empathy for others, no remorse, and no conscience be defined other than pure evil? Since science has failed to provide concrete proof as to what creates a Narcissist/sociopath, it's time to look somewhere else that might provide the answers. Maybe we are seeking answers in the wrong place and should take a serious look at the spiritual aspect.

Many victims of Narcissist abuse have had his/her faith tested or lost it all together. At one point, I was stripped of my belief and I denied the existence of God. After years of healing from having my soul raped by a Narcissist, I began dating a highly spiritual woman whom helped return my belief in God and introduced me to Reverend Larry Deason (author of Creation vs. Evolution). During one of our meetings, Larry pointed out that not all people have the possibility of ever making their way to heaven because God does in fact create some for destruction. **Romans 9:22** *What if, God, willing to show his wrath, and to make his power known, endured with much longsuffering the vessels of wrath fitted to destruction?* (The word "vessel" refers to humans.) When Larry read that passage, I immediately associated it with the existence of Narcissists and became driven to dig deeper. This could be the missing piece to the puzzle.

People created for destruction may not make sense to some because many of us are taught that God loves all his children, regardless of his/her behavior. We are told that all can be saved, but that is far from the truth and can be seen throughout the bible, as in **Isaiah 45:7** *"I form the light, and create darkness: I make peace, and create evil: I the LORD do all these things."* A few passages later, there is further confirmation that not all created will be saved. **Isaiah 54:16** (GW) *"... I've also created destroyers to bring destruction."* Wow! Stop right here. This clearly says that not all people have the capability of being good, and that God does, in fact, create evil. What does a Narcissist bring to anyone that gets close to him or her? Complete Destruction!

Does God purposely alter the makeup of certain people? Yes he does! This is proven in several Bible passages such as, **John 12:40** *"He has blinded their eyes and he hardened their heart, so that they would not see with their eyes and perceive with their heart."* This passage indicates that God blinds and hardens selected people, preventing them from recognizing the truth and stripping them of love. Before I go any further, let me ask you, "What is love?" God is love. What is the forefront trait of a Narcissist? It's the lack empathy and are incapability to loving anyone but them self. They are void of true love, which means they are stripped of God.

Narcissists are viewed as being soulless creatures, but how can that be? Are we not taught to believe that all men and women have a soul? If you believe this, once again, you would be wrong. Rev. Larry Deason undeniably proved in his book "Creation vs. Evolution" that there were two forms of humans on the earth when Adam and Eve was created, and that we are not all descendants of Adam and Eve. Adam and Eve were the first to been given souls, which meant there was an entire race without souls. This supposedly changed with Noah and the great flood that destroyed all life except what was on the Ark, after which people believe that only those with a soul roamed the earth. This would mean that all people, including the Narcissist have a soul. Let us take a deeper look below what's seen on the surface before coming up with a conclusion.

Noah's sons brought wives onboard the Ark with them, and although it says that the women were sanctified by their husbands, it does not prove that they were those living with a soul. This could mean that the chain of the soulless continued after the flood.

Therefore, it is possible that the soulless survived and walk the earth today.

If you've done any research, you've probably asked how and why narcissism is so widespread. The Bible refers to what may very well be causing the current Narcissist epidemic. **2 Timothy 3:1** *"But understand this, that in the last days there will come times of difficulty. For people will be lovers of self, lovers of money, proud, arrogant, abusive, disobedient to their parents, ungrateful, unholy, heartless, unappeasable, slanderous, without self-control, brutal, not loving good, treacherous, reckless, swollen with conceit, lovers of pleasure rather than lovers of God, having the appearance of godliness, but denying its power. Avoid such people."* Did you get all that? If not, look again. This scripture gives an accurate description of a Narcissist. There is no question about it, God created evil, and now it is clear to see that God created the Narcissist. I love the last sentence in that passage that is a warning and stresses that we avoid these wicked people.

Here is where it gets tricky. There are two types of Narcissists. One completely denies the existence of God, and the other claims (lies) to know God and have

again with all my heart. Those deep scares are no longer and I'm able to love with more passion than ever before. In *Ghost Of A Rose* I explain in detail what I did to be free from the agony.

Sources of reference on Narcissism

Malignant Self Love: Narcissism Revisited by Sam Vaknin Ph.D.

Without Conscience by Robert Hare Ph.D.

The Sociopath Next Door by Martha Stout

Narcissistic Personality Disorder by Kent Glowinski

The Narcissism Epidemic: Living in the Age of Entitlement by Jean M.Twenge and W. Keith Campbell

The Object of My Affection Is in My Reflection: Coping with Narcissists by Rokelle Lerner

So. You're in Love With a Narcissist by Alexandra Nouri

Narcissistic Lovers: How to Cope, Recover, and Move On by Cynthia Zayn & Kevin Dibble M.S.

Emotional Vampires by Albert Bernstein

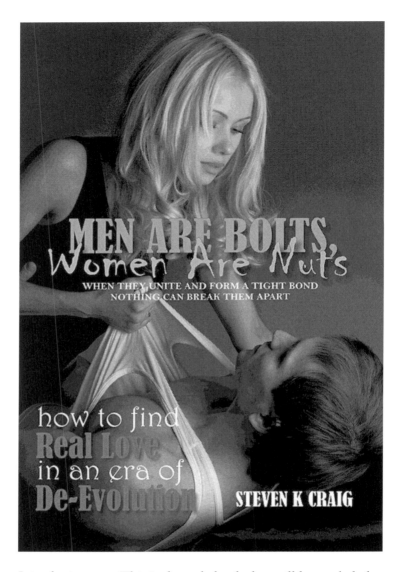

MEN ARE BOLTS,
Women Are Nuts

WHEN THEY UNITE AND FORM A TIGHT BOND
NOTHING CAN BREAK THEM APART

how to find
Real Love
in an era of
De-Evolution

STEVEN K CRAIG

Join the journey. This is the only book that will honestly help
you find the love of your life.

STEVEN K CRAIG

LITTLE MISS
DANGEROUS
BASED ON A TRUE STORY

Being Naughty Has Never Felt So Good.

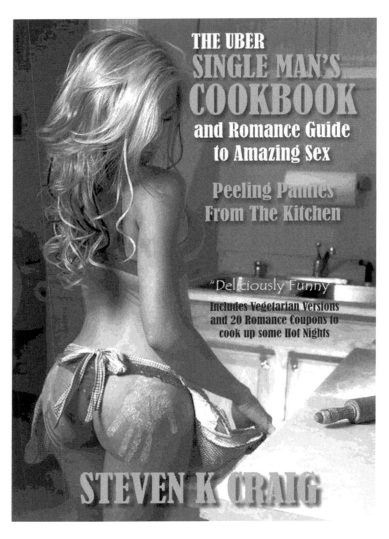

THE UBER
SINGLE MAN'S
COOKBOOK
and Romance Guide
to Amazing Sex

Peeling Panties
From The Kitchen

"Deliciously Funny"

Includes Vegetarian Versions
and 20 Romance Coupons to
cook up some Hot Nights

STEVEN K CRAIG

The best present a woman can give herself is gifting this book
to her man. A book every man should own.

Books by Steven K Craig
available at www.steven-k-craig.com

L.O.V.E IS A FOUR LETTER WORD QUADRILOGY

GHOST OF A ROSE
A delightfully disturbing romance. The only memoir on Narcissism from beginning to end in real time as it took place. Oh yes... there will be tears.

MEN ARE BOLTS, Women Are Nuts
The quest to find real love in an era of de-evolution. Written in George Carlin style of humor and the only book that WILL find you true love.

Little Miss Dangerous
If 50 Shades of Grey got your panties damp, this one will melt them right off your flesh. Based on a true story.

The Uber Single Man's Cookbook and Romance Guide to Amazing Sex
Every man should own this book. The best present a woman could give herself is giving this book to her man.

Author Steven K Craig

Steven K Craig has led an amazing life. He was the original manager and co-creator of the iconic heavy metal band Slayer. He left the music industry to pursue a career in art and became world renowned for his talent with the airbrush and graphic arts as the owner of SKC Customz. His creative mind brought forth one of the first interactive digital magazines "Airbrushtechlive" and has written for many art publications including Airbrush Action Magazine. His other books include "Ghost of a Rose" and "Men Are Bolts, Women Are Nuts."

Visit his website www.steven-k-craig.com

13616594R00045

Made in the USA
San Bernardino, CA
31 July 2014